seaglass picnic

with a splash of post traumatic Stress

seaglass picnic

with a splash of post traumatic Stress

Frances Driscoll

Published by
Pleasure Boat Studio: A Literary Press

Seaglass Picnic, by Frances Driscoll

ISBN 978-0-912887-41-8
Library of Congress Control Number: 2015951364

First U.S. Printing

Design by Susan Ramundo
Cover by Lauren Grosskopf

Pleasure Boat Studio books are available through your favorite bookstore and
through SPD (Small Press Distribution), Partners/West, Baker & Taylor,
Ingram, Brodart, Amazon.com, and bn.com.

and also through our website via credit card:
PLEASURE BOAT STUDIO: A LITERARY PRESS
www.pleasureboatstudio.com
201 West 89th Street
New York, NY 10024
pleasboat@nyc.rr.com

Gratefully acknowledgement is made to Vice Versa Press which printed
a broadside of *The Eaten Heart*.

for

Andy & Aileen

for

Janet & Donald

for

Elizabeth

for

My Ocean

Contents

The Eaten Heart

for Andrew Long (March 25, 1962–March 19, 2014)

Roma historian Sarah Carmona says in Romani
when you want to tell someone you love him
you might say,
I eat your heart.

Love,
I have eaten your heart.

And,

you,
my beloved,
have eaten mine.

seaglass
picnic

Train/Trains. Peach Melba.

Way to school
the word
train
is
in the lyrics.

Train is a name for gang rape.
I try not to think about that.
I've got a lane change to make soon coming
so I can't think about that. Now.
Sound safely now off
I think about other trains &
being in one with
someone beside me so no bad stuff is
going to get me.
Maybe, we are in a train going
from or to
Paris.
If from
we'll have Peach Melba
before leaving.
If to
we'll have Peach Melba
upon arriving.
Hope to.
They have such lovely there hotels.

Men/Peaches. Peaches/Men.

It works,
Molly says.

Dip them in boiling water.
Then, into a cold ice bath in the sink.
And, the skin slides right off.

I think
Molly is talking about men.

Molly is talking about
peaches.

Red Sticker Fragile

They also have
Red
Fragile
Stickers.

But,
those,
they have to pay for.

So,
they can't just
give
those away.
Not
even
one
of
those
Red
Fragile
Stickers. Away.

So,
if
you happen upon
one
or
even
two
of
those
Red
Fragile
Stickers

Save. Keep.

Look at now and then.
Think of. Remember
someone you know/love
who may be feeling
a little Fragile.
Red Sticker Fragile.
Today.

In fact,
right now,
close your eyes.
Let us all close all of our eyes.
Now. Here. Together.
Think of someone we/you/me
know is feeling a little somewhat
Fragile right now.
Red Sticker Fragile.

to go properly into the past

The Earth Observatory researcher says,
to go properly into the past,
you can drill an ice core.

Tools of her trade:
a contractor's saw and a tape measure.

In my house,
I can never find the tape measure.
And, of course, I have no idea what
a contractor's saw is.

But,
I do know one good way
to go properly into the past:
Have yourself a little post traumatic stress episode.
One that comes with flashbacks.
Lots of flashbacks.

after over 26 years

it begins
before school outside
smoking coffee writing

Colleen comes by
I've been reading your book
it's very intense

she stands there standing there
he had his hands around my throat
he had his hands around my throat
he had his hands around my throat

if she says it again if she says it again if she says it again
she says it many more times

then says
you can write my story
you can write my story

do not go to school
do not call in

it begins
it has begun

Andy tells me
No. No, Hon.
That is not the beginning.
I am the beginning.

Yes, of course. Of course.
Andy is the beginning.

Andy Finds Me

Andy finds me.
We share school memory, years of new news,
poems, poems.

Begins to tell me his story.
Age 8. The male babysitter.
It's a game, he told Andy.

The long dead life after since.

Andy is mine.

This is different than
the anonymous strangers
whose stories I hold.

This is different.

Things People Want To Know

Liz wants to know
Did I find any poems in the newspaper today.

Tha wants to know
How I am holding up.

Andy wants to know
Do I believe in God.

Ocean wants to know
Why it is now nap time.

Me & Sally Don't Think Alike

Sally comes home.

Sal, I say,
Just talked with Myrna.
Told her I need to take a 2-week medical leave.
Due to this small little episode.
Re-occurrence of post traumatic stress.

Oh, no,
Sally says,
Oh, Honey, why.
Why did you say that.
Why, why didn't you just say
you are having a hysterectomy.
Will be out 6 weeks.

Ocean's Career

Dragons.
That's my job.

I'm a dragon trainer.

How do you train a dragon, Ocean.

You fly with the dragon.

Ocean,
how many dragons have you trained.

Eighteen.

Well,
actually
one.

What Is/What If

(*A Law & Order: Special Victims Unit Poem*)

Think about What Is,
Andy says.
You do not need to be concerned with
What If.

What If
is
Quicksand.

Olivia and Andy think alike.

Her scriptwriters forgetting we are already dead,
Olivia tells a Law & Order: Special Victims Unit victim,
The What Ifs Will Kill You.

But, I know how to deal with Quicksand.

Do Not Move.

Facing death. I learned.
Not To Move.

Plot.

I love amnesia.

It's my favorite.

Along with nun-leaving-the-convent memoirs.

It's not a rape thing.

I have always loved amnesia.

My Ocean's Painting

My Ocean sends me a painting.

Well, really his mother sends.
His mother writes in a note
the painting's title:
1 Hat, 2 H's, and Some Flowers.

There are in fact 3 H's.
The H's are bright pink.
There is
a big H
a medium size H
and
a one wee small H.

(My Ocean has been reading
Goldilocks and the Three Bears.)

There are also two
bright blue scribbles.
The small scribble
is
(I imagine)
the hat
the larger blue scribble
is
(I imagine)
some flowers.

Why we watch.

(A Law & Order: Special Victims Unit Poem)

I read this long poem I write
to my sister
about why rape victims
and I am one
watch
Law & Order: Special Victims Unit.

After I read my long poem
about why rape victims
and I am one
watch
Law & Order: Special Victims Unit.

My sister says
has the cast changed much over the years.

Mating Fish Hum

(A Headline Poem)

Well,

doesn't everybody.

Needing Recess

We have now lost over 50 minutes of recess,
Sam, 9-going-on-59, says.
because They, yes, They will not stop
Talking and Moving.

Oh, Sam, I say, I am so sorry.
When children can not stop
talking and can not stop moving,
that is exactly when they need recess.

I know that, Sam says. I know
when children need recess.

Newly Open.

Outside waiting outside for my dear friend.
We are going as always out for breakfast food.
I see a man I do not know have
before never seen around about.
He sees me. I see him see me.
Begin to walk toward me
I like before freeze in absolute
terror. Standing still try to hide myself.
Know there is no escape from what
is about to happen.
Ari is saying my name.
He steadies me until
I can stand walk on my own.
That I do not recognize him
this worries him.
Worries me more.

Donald says,
this is normal.
Newly opened/opening eyes
are almost always blind.
Everything is unfamiliar to a baby.

I do not find this helpful.

Cuts & Bleeding

Honey, please, Andy says,
do not cut or burn yourself today.

I think I read this somewhere
maybe I made it up but
this is what happened to me so
what I think I somewhere read is
sometimes the pain center(s?)
shutdown
&
sometimes the pain center(s?)
regenerate & sometimes
they don't
they don't
is what has happened so far to me at least not
almost 27 years yet later
clumsy
have always cut myself cutting chopping
burnt myself cooking ironing
but since
the cuts the burns
more severe I do not
realize I am hurt until I am
real hurt or I do not
at all realize a day or days
later I see my useless hands &
& wonder what has happened how
did that happen

Liz is helping me organize my
papers books hard to do with a
person who does so crave love disorder
disarray she leaves the room comes back in
I am in short shorts sitting sorting
Honey Liz says
you are bleeding
I look down
my right inner thigh covered with blood
my right hand lower right arm
Liz says Honey
I say Liz
I'll explain later
get peroxide
band-aids
from above my outer right wrist
a gash pours blood
when it happened I was
there but felt nothing no
idea how banged up & other stuff I
was until the rape doctor wanted
answers I did not have
now I keep on ready hand
peroxide extra strength antibiotic cream band-aids
lots of band-aids

Liz discovers among papers, books
a black knee-length tags-still-on skirt
oh I say that's my emergency funeral skirt
Honey Liz says you have
an emergency funeral skirt
yes I say I do yes
yes

Things Healthy Women Do Differently

(A Headline Poem)

Bet one thing is:

Not get themselves raped.

Sister Talk

Do you think I've had a mini stroke,
Sal says.

No, I say,
could be early alzheimer's symptoms.

Thanks Hon, Sal says.

Looking/Not looking: For

Looking up some obituary stuff of a poet
I love who is now newly dead.

Instead
I somehow
happen upon
two articles about rape.
1. 2 women, 36 & 24 gang raped brutally in at dusk a park
2. some young teenage boys by some older teenage boys raped
    at a soccer sports camp

One happened in Delaware.
One, Massachusetts.

I forget all about looking for my dead poet obituary.

Go outside.
And, in the courtyard
seated. Sip some red wine.
Some cheap and bitter red wine.

Andy's Idea of Good Advice

My sister Sally is
pan-frying canned chick peas
she is planning to eat.

Andy says,
Don't think about it.
Don't worry about it.
And, don't look.

Andy hopes

I am dreaming

of

seaglass

and

of

sponge cake

I am dreaming

of

Minefields

Andy has to be so careful with me.

He cannot write, say
This word or That word.
Andy has to be careful with me.

"It is a trick,"
Andy says,
"to use
perfectly innocent language
because
you never know
when you are
stepping
on a
Minefield."

For example,
Andy,
yes,
perfectly innocently,
says,
"I am combing through our poems.
Combing through our letters."

Comb equals Minefield.

And, I remember.
A comb. Another kind of combing.

A comb that is used for another purpose.
A terrible purpose.

Andy steps on Minefields all the time.

Endnote:
During the rape exam the examining doctor
combs
(Yes!)
victim pubic hair
seeking evidence
of other hair.

Baby, Baby

He says the word
Baby.
Maybe speaking of his youngest.
My baby girl
Baby is a Minefield word.
I react.

Seldom,
he says
have I ever used that word with a woman
And,
I would not use that word with you.

I wonder why he would not use that word with me.
What words would he use.
Oh, no, he doesn't talk does he.
Talk while lovemaking. That makes it just
impossible to concentrate. (As, in,
oh, dear, what am I supposed to be doing now.)

But, it would maybe be ok by me. If
he did use that word. If he whispered to me:
Baby, Baby, Oh Baby.
Because I would just begin laughing and
laughing. And, he would begin laughing.
And, we would be in bed just laughing. Laughing
in bed. And

The Definition of Fragile.

What he says.

What she thinks he means
when he says that.

I meant sensitive, he says.
Not fragile.

As I Minefield Spell react to
fragile.
As sounds like to me a girl.
Something a girl might be.
Fragile. Delicate. Feminine.
And, I so do not want to be any of those things.
And, of course, I do want to be all of those things.
Especially the one most untrue.

Fragile, I obsess react.
Someone fragile enough she breaks.
Someone fragile enough she is so easy to break.
She is already broken.

Not breakable, he says, just sensitive.

I meant sensitive, he says, again.
As we have to go through this twice or more.
So he says right away again
I meant sensitive.

You are an astonishing woman, he says.

At first to the word
astonishing, I react
to that of course badly.
I'm ordinary, I say. Mundane.
I do wish
I could be perceived to be interesting.
You are, he says. You are interesting.

But then the next day
it is to the word woman, I Minefield Spell react.
I would so much prefer if instead he used the word
person.

I hate to think of him thinking of me as a woman.
If I must be something I would rather be a person.
I don't want to be a woman. Anymore.
I was never any good at being a woman anyway so
being a person might be ok if you have to be
something.

You are fragile.
Not he says, as in breakable.
As in sensitive.

But I think he means very breakable and
maybe that is true because I am that
fragile. That breakable. That

He is right. Fragile is the right word. And not
in the sense of sensitive. We both know sensitive is/was a kind lie because
he is kind to me.

Small slivers fragments only still now yes yet remain
of a broken woman. I am now only remnants,
bits, slices, teeth-bitten thread too shredded
to catch inside any need eye.

He's right. Fragile is the right word.
And, the definition of fragile is
breakable. Broken.

He takes off his shirt.

He did.
He does this.
He took off his shirt.
But,
that's not really the point.
The point is he told me.
He told me.
He is taking off his shirt.
Hold on a sec, Hon, he says.
I'm taking my shirt off.
You're taking off your shirt, I,
maybe,
say.
It's ok, Hon, he says,
I have on an undershirt.
Well,
thank god he has on an undershirt.
But,
why did he tell me he is
taking off his shirt.
I'm a rape victim and
I'm having a small. Little. Well kind of bad
re-occurrence
of post traumatic stress and
the last thing I now need is to think
about, visualize, a man
taking off his shirt.
Even if,
he does have on an undershirt.
Because, then, of course,

I have to visualize the undershirt.
The undershirt with him in it.
And,
I am frightened, scared, frightened
even though, even though, even though
and, but, oh, even though he is I know
a man but he is a man
who
I love
and
feel safe with
and
who
I know
believe
with all of my heart
will/would/will never hurt me
(hurt means rape) (hurt is another word for rape)
even though
sometimes
he has to remind me
of those things
remind me
of that
Hon, you're safe, Hon, he says, Hon, you are
Hon, safe with me.
Hon, I will never hurt you. Hon, he says, Hon
I will never hurt you.
At least,
he is wearing an undershirt.
Can you imagine if
I had had to visualize
bare male skin above the waist.
Well,

bare male skin anywhere really.

Not now.

Not now.

And,

perhaps

probably

most likely

never.

And,

that's ok, that's ok.

And,

we are talking on the telephone.

He is far up the northeast coast.

Well, the northeast.

Not really the coast.

He is more inland,

near one of those maybe lakes or.

And,

I am here.

And,

there is no reason to be so afraid

when a man says on the telephone

I am taking off my shirt.

But,

I'm as I said having this

little post traumatic stress thing going on

right now and

I am thinking

why did he tell me this

on the telephone.

He could have taken off his shirt

and

I would have never have known.

So, why,
when he knows I am now feeling
the way I am now feeling
why did he tell me this.
Why did he tell me
he is taking off his shirt.

Hon, Honey, Hon.
My social worker cousin Janet says,
any one can make a mistake.

The shirt I saw him take off is the pale
pink one.
Later, he tells me, the shirt is blue.

I think for a woman maybe most
every woman
a blue shirt is safer. Don't you think.
Maybe, I would not have been so scared
if I had known the shirt he is taking off is
the blue one.

That pink one. The pale pink one. I'm real
afraid of that pale pink one. Well, isn't
most every woman. Afraid. Afraid of that
pale pink shirt. I think so. I think
we are all afraid of that pale pink
shirt. We all know
what could/might happen. We all know.
We know.

Go to bed

Go to bed is a strange phrase,
Andy says.
I really don't find it all that strange myself, but
maybe the phrase means something different to
Andy
than it does to me.
To me, it means, a child
going to bed and actually sleeping through the night.
I wonder what it does mean to Andy.
Not that I'm thinking of asking.
Not any time soon.

Yes, he probably should have.

What is the problem you are having,
Donald says.

I begin to cry.
(without of course actual tears)

Probably, if I had phrased that
a little differently, he says.

Is there a problem you are having.

There is. There is. Really
really a problem. Really.

All right. Well. Well.
Let's define that.

The Cry-Outs

For years, my sister, niece have been saying in the night in bed
I cry out.
As in
last night you cried out in your sleep.

For years, I've assume one cry-out, maybe two cry-outs.

A this morning January,
my mother says,
Did you have a difficult night.
I maybe shrug. Say nothing.
Have no night memory.
My mother continues.
You screamed from midnight until 3 am.
I say nothing.

Phone Liz. Say Liz,
tell me about the cry-outs.
Liz, do I scream for hours.

Yes, Honey, Liz says,
you scream for hours.
One scream. Two minutes later. Five minutes later.
One minute later. Ten minutes later. Three minutes
later. For hours.

But, Honey, Liz says, it's
only twice or so a week.

Lillian Wants To Know

(A Law & Order: Special Victims Unit Poem)

Q & A Revolution Berkeley Books
Lillian wants to know
why
I use in a poem
(about why Rape Victims watch
Law & Order: Special Victims Unit)
the word victim.

Because it's true, Lillian.
Because we are, Lillian.
We are victims, Lillian,
of a terrible crime, Lillian.
We are, Lillian, crime victims, Lillian.

Lillian.
It's not
Law & Order: Special Survivors Unit.
Lillian.

And, Lillian, that's ok, Lillian.
There is nothing wrong, Lillian,
with, Lillian, the truth.

End,
she comes up to me.
Whispers.
I watch Law & Order: Special Victims Unit.
Everybody tells me I shouldn't.

We all watch it, Lillian. We all do.

First, she dreams. Then, she begins to write.

The night of the day,
I fly to my assaulted girlchild,
she dreams she is pregnant.
Next day, she begins to write
about the assault & about after the assault.
She's writing about it. She is writing about it.
Now.

Airport Re-Enactment

How to freeze
not move
I am instructed
not to move
Instructed how to move
This has happened
before
to me
once before
I was instructed not to move
instructed how to move
not to move
I remember

this airport woman is
only interested in
my small left breast
he wasn't much interested
in my small breasts
he was real interested
in
my
down there
real interested
I remember
Re-Remember.

Forgetting/Remembering Why

Long lovely lunching in the Hotel Durant,
before our Revolution reading,
we sit at a big round table
facing one another.
Not speaking. Each of us writing.
Writing about rape.

Don't you love this, I say.
I'm so glad I came.

Yes, I love this, Aileen says.
I'm so glad you came.

It's changed my life, I say.
(No idea what I mean by that.)
Mine, too, Aileen says.
(No idea what she means by that.)

Then,
we look into one another's eyes.
Remember.
Why I am here.
Why I came.

Both of us look fast down.
Close our eyes for a minute.
Start writing again.
Writing about rape.

My first hug from Andy.

Andy phones Revolution
before our reading
wishes Aileen luck
it is her first bookshop reading
tells Aileen
after the reading and only
if you think Honey can handle it
give her a hug
and after and only
if you think Honey can handle it
tell her
the hug is from me

lunching next day
but Aileen I say
how did he know to say that
yes Aileen says
yes
how did he know

Andy just knows. Knows me. Andy knows.

That Object

I'd really kind of pretty much well
actually forgotten all about
that object and about what that
object looks like and now
I kind of do remember
what they sort of look like

really wish
I did not remember

And
you know how when
you start thinking about something
you just can't stop thinking about
the something.

9 words.

This is what happens. How it happens.

Andy begins to read my the rape poems.

Says to me.

If you could be held,
I would hold you.

9 words.
I crash/sink deep down
into post traumatic stress episode.
9 words.

About a maybe week later.
I am saying to Donald,
Do you think I need to be hospitalized.
Donald says to me,
Do you think you need to be hospitalized.

I do not find this helpful.

I talk with Andy. Tell him everything/anything
I find this helpful.

Fishing. Fishing.

Fishing in my drink,
I fish out
Two Blueberries.

Two Blueberries,
I exclaim.

That changes everything,
Aileen explains,
to our waitress.
That changes everything.

Our Revolution reading
about to begin,
I ceremonially unwrap
the Hotel Durant
blueberry holding napkin.

Blueberries on our tongues,
Fishing for far more than Grace,
eyes into eyes
together
we swallow.

My neighbor Colleen's sister Trish says.

Stress and pain make you age.

Always put sunblock on your lips.

Keep a fishing knife in your bag.

My niece keeps a fishing knife in her car.
By the emergency brake.
For easy access.

She says,
I've let it rust.
So when I stab,
he gets a terrible infection.

If you give the blade a little twist
as you stab,
the wound will not close.
He will bleed out.

I like that very much,
she says, smiling.

Choice. But, we don't get to choose.

My neighbor,
That young, beautiful, blonde girl,
You know the criminology professor,
The one with the Wheaten Terrier I'd like to kidnap,
Up for this fall
Tenure,
She has studied
a lot
about this.

I'd rather be murdered,
she says,
than raped.

But, we don't get to choose.
If, later, we want death,
we have to murder ourselves.
There are a lot of ways to do that.
I know some of them.

Some of the ways I know take a long time.
A real long time.
You want my list.
My list includes:
Lack of exercise. Red Meat. Cigarettes.
Loss of both night & peripheral vision. Irish whiskey.
Neat.

Saying the Words

I love you
I tell him
all the time
over and over
I love you.

Believe
he really needs
to hear that know that
believe himself much
loved.

One day
these
hideous
mangled
strangled
sounds
choke
their way out of him.

He is saying to me for the first time
I love you.

A Taste of Honey

Mum gets a gift.

Gourmet lip balm.
Named
a taste of honey.

Mum gives it
to me.

I give it
to Andy.

My little girl warrior queen

In,
at least,
one,
past life,
she was,
I know,
a warrior queen.
Still carries and still holds
that
regal bearing.
Her neck
so slender
and
so long.

And,
now,
here,
in this life,
who will she
lead into battle.
And,
for
what,
what,
now,
here,
in this life
will she
fight.

The One Story I Know

(a newspaper found poem)

Pierced by sorrow so keen it seemed
inconceivable all she had to show
for (over) 20 passed by years was/is
these scattered reminders.

I know that story.

I know everything about all about
that story.

New Alum Chum

Lunching with a just met also 1987 rape girl
much younger than me.
She mentions having a baby after.
How did you do that, I say.
I can't imagine how you were able to do that.
Well, she says,
it wasn't easy.
Took me over 25 years.

We laugh. We both laugh. Can't stop.

January 8.

Wednesday. January 8, 2014.
Salmon River Waterfalls Freeze.
This happens in the Winter months.
Ice-Climbing the frozen falls is a popular activity.

Wednesday. January 8, 2014.
Is the Second Anniversary of Daisy's Rape.

Sunday. January 8, 2012.
Dumped after the Party in her Own Yard's Snow.
Found by her Own Mother Left for Dead.
Without coat. Without shoes.
Freezing. Ice chunks in her hair.

"I am Different Now . . . My Whole Life since January 8, 2012 has been
a Long Reckless Winter . . . I am Different Now."

One way she is different now is she is
no longer blonde.

Sunday. January 5, 2014.
Is the 3rd time Daisy tries to kill herself.

Her weather reports Dangerous
Cold. High Wind. Ice.
This happens in the Winter months.

Leftover dreams & more
inside a small yellow butterfly world.

A sunflower may just stand all day straight,
leaning, looking
into the sun & the heat.
It's a quiet, peaceful life.
Not exactly intellectual or social but
quiet & nice.

But,
a small, yellow butterfly
does she have to keep flying all
around, all over, all about or
can she take time now & again to rest
in inside within a leaf just rest &
dream of what small yellow butterflies dream
of sun clouds, late afternoon fancy cut jam sandwiches with
clotted cream, bright blue leather belts & other expensive
accessories, paper clips in various sizes, priority mail, French
perfume preferably free samples of French perfume, romance
novels featuring amnesia, high thread count all white all
cotton bed linens, a newly discovered previously unseen
episode of sex & the city in which everyone orgasms
including that one, longhair marmalade kittens, fuzzy any
color socks, open face all Danish butter crust hand picked wild
blueberry pies & of course in a small yellow butterfly world
there is no sexual violence. And, love. Well, it's possible. In
a small yellow butterfly world pretty much anything is, don't you
think possible, don't you imagine. Even, elbows. And, even

That conversation.

She is beside me
writing on Ann's deck
by the redwood
what she will say to tell
her mother.

She stops.
Looks up.
At me.
Do I also have to tell her
I like girls.

As
she is dead serious
I too
have to be
dead serious.

Imagine that conversation.
Mummy
I am calling to tell you June 5
I was sexually assaulted
and
also
by the way
I like girls.

p.s.

Matt is in Missouri in college.
Daisy is in Missouri in a psychiatric hospital.

(Repeat.)

(Repeat.)

Several Harps Stolen From Nevada City Harpist Home

(A Headline Poem)

(Not real good form to end
a headline with a preposition but)

remember
that little blonde girl
who got herself kidnapped
out of her own bedroom
at night
by a real bad pedophile
And it was all over TV
she was very white very blonde
and was missing for a long time
later found
so called alive
well she played the harp
I wonder if she still plays the harp

um. yeah.

hon
find this fascinating sweet
talking about rape, poetry
during revolution q&a
aileen charms me
adopts my custom
our sentences drift off
both end our driftings
saying
um yeah
i am you know famous for this
she is my daughter
home soon
love
hon

Me & Elizabeth

She does still
play the harp.

Now, in hotel lobbies.

In public talks
about rape, sexual abuse, torture, abduction
she says
do not let
your past
define
Your Future.

Does rape
define
you,
Andy says.

I say,
I don't
know
what you mean.

A Puritan Girl

I'm from Massachusetts and so a
yes Puritan and yes we
all vote for any and all Kennedys
but
we don't use words
like that.

Although, yes.
I had heard of that word,
I had never heard that word.
Certainly never said myself that word.

The first therapy go-around
with Donald he wanted
to know what the word is.
I could not. Could not possibly
say that word.
Could you write it.
No. I could not. Could not possibly
write that word.
I know I had to put up with a lot
with his metaphors and stuff. But
he had to put up with a lot too.

First time
I heard that word
was
when Ray the/my Rapist
said

You have a pretty pussy.
I'm touching your pussy.
Do you like the way I'm touching your pretty pussy.

After that,
I really did not like that word.

And, in this episode,
I begin to re-remember him
saying that word.
And, I keep re-remembering.

But, then,
along with the you know episode
there is all this this coming alive again stuff
and I am coming alive everywhere
including down there.
But, being a Puritan and from Massachusetts,
am without language so
Janet explains about the vulva.
Had no idea what
the vulva is. Never heard actually of that.
The vulva you know has 5 parts. Imagine that.
Andy who likes being my research assistant
sends me a long long long list of vulva words.
Lots are pretty funny.
Cha Cha I find most adorable.
Then I got to I guess thinking
and
I thought. I thought.
Pussy. Pussy. Pussy.
Pussy is not a terrible word.

It's not. Andy, I say, pussy is not
a terrible word. Pussy is a sweet word.
Yes, Andy says, pussy is a sweet word.
A sweet word.

Andy Dictates A List

Andy dictates a list
to me
of stuff
I could use
to touch my own body with.
I think it was a good list.
I of course misplace the list.
I don't know what I've done with the list.
It's somewhere in this house, I know.
The list remains misplaced.

I think it was
in my memory, a real good list.
Imaginative, quirky, fun.
Stuff actually likely to work.

My body remains untouched.

Jam. Pickles. Brussel Sprouts.

He agrees.
I will never like jelly.

But,
there are all these foods I have never
tasted he thinks I might/may/will like/love.
We make a list.

Where To Begin.
Jam.
Pickles.
Brussel Sprouts.

Blackberry Jam, he says.

I've eaten blackberries.
Me and Grammy Driscoll used to pick sun warm plump and wild
blackberries in the wood behind her house.

Pickles.
He says Dill and Bread and Butter.

Grandpa Driscoll used to make
his own pickles.
From the cucumbers he grew in his sideyard summer garden.

Brussel Sprouts.

I have been very much interested in brussel sprouts all this past year because
in the serial killer mysteries I like to read

in nice restaurants the detectives have all been ordering
brussel sprouts and so I have been wondering about them.

Sauté in garlic, Andy says.
Lemon, I say.
Lemon is good, Andy says. Lemon is always good.

Normal/Not Normal

Father Kelly says this is normal
Donald says this is normal
They're both just plain loon crazy
I know this is
not
normal
I know that
and I have to do it
I'm the one who has to do it
Once a week I have
to do it
and it makes me sick to my stomach
and
I can barely stand doing it
It's so awful
and it makes me so sick to my stomach
and I have to do it
Because we do not have
any full service gas stations
anymore
So I have to do it
myself
And I try to remember to do it
on Sunday
but I never do
So usually there's enough gas left
in the car to get me
to school Monday morning
and I can get it then at the Texaco station
right by school on the way home

and get lemonade if I want.
But sometimes
I have to do it at the Shell station
by home
and that's no way for me to start
any day
and it makes me sick
I never liked doing it
But since this post traumatic stress
little episode
has come upon me
it's so
and I know it's not normal
and Donald refuses to prescribe
me anything
and Andy says well Honey
I'd worry about prescribing
you anything too
so I have to do it and
hold in my left hand this terrible
huge penis like object and
Insert
Hate the word insert, hate to insert
which reminds me of that other word
I can't now think about
but I am now thinking about
penetration
hate that word, hate thinking, about
that word, hate thinking about penetration
once before there was, a time, I actually liked
the feel of that
can't imagine that now
And I have to hold it in my

left hand and insert it in, into, inside
the small round open
vagina like object
and it's so awful
and you can't believe how long it
takes to pump
hate that word too
reminds me of real bad stuff
and it takes so long to get
twenty dollars worth of gas
in, into, inside this gray car
and I hate the color gray
but it was the only cheap used
Chevrolet the Chevrolet place had
and you can't believe how hard it was with my credit to get that
car loan when I came home from China.
and I know it's not normal
not normal at all
and sometimes both Father Kelly and Donald
are both just fucking useless, useless.

Does anybody here have a spare Xanax.

Lunch with Sunflower Wishes

Lunchtime trying
some bibliotherapy
some unconditional love therapy
some Happy Sunflower Wish Therapy
with
my two small 1st grade ones
Cal & Zack

They eat
while
I read
Ferdinand the Bull

Skip run
slide fast down slides

Find small yellow flowers
they call Sunflowers
tangle all up in my hair

Visit with our courtyard Sunflower

The Sunflower means Happiness
they know
Cal & Zack take turns watering her
Slowly Carefully Gently
We close eyes
Make silent Happy Sunflower Wishes
Share our wishes

Calvin's today wish
I wish Zack gets back on green
Zack's today wish
I wish a 2nd pair of shoes

My wish
Lunch Tomorrow
with
my Cal my Zack

Bob is not the right answer.

The Tester Woman
testing 4-year-olds
testing for school readiness
says: Point.
Point to the picture of the bird
who comes out at night and
says Who.
The child points.
Points to the owl.
The Tester Woman
gives the child
points.
Points for correct pointing.
So, then, the Tester Woman
says
So,
what is the name of that bird.
Bob,
the child says.
The Tester Woman
shakes her head.
Gives that response
no points.
Zero points.
Bob is not
the answer
the Tester Woman
wants.
I think
Bob

is
an excellent A+ answer.
That is why
I am not
a Tester Woman.

No Arms. No Hands.

First Grade Zach makes
a paper cut-out portrait
of his father.

Excellent cutting, Zach, I say.
Excellent glueing, Zach, I say.
Beautiful portrait, Zach, I say.

Zach's portrait of his father has
No arms. No hands.

Dealing with Disaster

If you are on fire:
Drop and Roll.

If you are buried in rubble:
Tap.

We know all about disaster.
You can ask us anything.

True Fact.
China.
Eastern Sichuan.
Earthquake.

Searchers searching for
any yet still alive child cried. Cried out.
Tap. Tap. If you can hear me.
If you can hear me. Tap. Tap.

There was as you so well remember
so little if any tapping.

There was much crying.

There is always much crying.

Inappropriate Laughter

1.

At least, he's eating, my sister says.
Oh, Thank God, I say, he's eating.

We both laugh. Can't stop.

Why are you laughing, Andy says.

All Driscoll girls have this problem
with uncontrollable inappropriate laughter.
It's awful and
why none of us could ever anchor
network tv evening news.
I don't know why. It's what we do.

Denial, Andy says. Denial.
Oh, I say. Oh. Denial.

2.

Liz is working on a Stress Management class project.
She has chosen post traumatic stress.
We find this amusing.

She finds film
of real people talking about their ptsd
symptoms and treatments.

I howl wet your pants howl laughing.

Oh, those poor people, I say.

Look at text list of symptoms.
You know, Liz, I say,
I still have a few of those.

Liz stares.
Hon, she says,
you have all of them.
Each and every single one of them.
All.

Well, I say, maybe some.
We laugh. We both laugh.

Zach Chats

1.

I can move my ears.

Oh, Zach, I can't.

I know.
You have to be a boy
and
a child.

2.

Oh, Zach,
my hair is a mess today.

Yes,
your hair is a mess today.

My Children

My wounded children are worried.
Tell their mothers.
She is not at school.
We do not know
where she is.

I talk on the telephone with my mothers.
Explain.
On little short medical leave.
Just a little episode.
Re-occurrence of post-traumatic stress.

But,
don't tell my children that.
Tell my children,
Soon. Soon.
I will be back in school.
I have not forgotten them.

My Neck/Anthony's Eyes

What happened to your neck,
2nd grade small & tears prone,
Anthony says.

Nothing happened to my neck, Anthony.
It's just an old neck, Anthony,
it doesn't hurt me.

Do you find it ugly to look at.
Does it bother you, Anthony, to look
at my neck.

No, it's ok. It does not bother me
to look at your neck. I don't
think your neck is ugly.
I just want to know
what happened to it.

Best Friends

You are so nice, Zach.
You are such a nice boy.

You be nice to me.
I be nice to you.
You are my best friend.

And, you, Zach,
you are my best friend.

Leaf Hunting

Whitney's Kindergarten is off on a Leaf Hunt

It's Magic, one girl says.
Magic, her friend agrees.

One boy shows me the flower in his hand.
(There is no flower in his hand.)

It disappeared, he says.
That's Magic, he says.

The Unfinished . . .

(a found poem)

The Unfinished unfinished
lure us
along a path
to understanding of
process, impulse.

The Unfinished are Unfinished
for any number of reasons
poverty or war
change of plan or vision
illness or death.

Might Be A Stretch

For years, mum has been saying,
Honey,
can't you write
a pleasant poem.
People like
to read
a pleasant poem.

I don't say anything.

A few days ago,
mum says,
I wish
you would not
write
about violence.
Violence is, I guess, her word for rape.

I don't say anything.

Today,
she says,
maybe,
you could
write
something about
suffering and pain.
Suffering and pain
must be her word
for something other than rape.

I don't say anything.

So,
Janet,
I say,
what do you think
do you think
I could write
something about
suffering and pain.

Oh, Hon,
Janet says,
it would be a stretch
but

Breathe, Hon. Hon, Breathe.

No idea now what set me off.
Likely a word of language.
But I am like
mad-woman hyperventilating
(And, boy, do I know how boy do I know
how to do that real good.)
in the midst of sad sorry to say yet yes
yes another after after after yes so
oh so many years
Panic Attack.

And you you just
in the kindest slowest most gentle calm yes
voice
say
Breathe, Hon. Hon, Breathe.
And
Somehow Somehow
I do
And
then
Everything Is All Right.
I am Breathing
And
Everything Is All Right
Now
Because.

Whispers

Andy likes to whisper,
He's good at it.
He really is.
Why, he's practically famous
for his whispers.

Let me tell you
some of Andy's best whispers:

Cucumbers. Cucumbers.
Oh, that's a really good one.
Might actually be his best.
Or definitely one of his best.

Puff pastry.
Poached eggs.
Low tide.
Waning moon.
Shampoo. Shampoo.
My name. My name. My name.

Meeting Jacob

Button cute & worryingly far too
thin, Jacob happens by trying
to sell AT&T stuff
as I am on my patio
writing,
smoking,
drinking awful cheap bad
red wine.
(I just force myself. When
your analyst will not give you
any Xanax it's the only thing
you can do so I do it I just
force myself. It does not really
work but one can hope.)
I print for him my name and telephone number.
He goes off. Comes back.
Are you, he says, Frances Driscoll
the writer of The Rape Poems.
I say, yes.
He says, The Rape Poems was required reading
my first semester Studio Art Class
at U Washington Seattle.
I say, Oh.
His eyes in this
just past dusk almost darkness
I have to ask. Hazel, he says. But,
I say, we both pretend they are green.
Yes, he says. And, we both say all
at once together
and, sometimes they are. They are

sometimes green.
Green is the color of safety.
Well, I guess that's sort of right.
I am still alive.

Sharing Our Plans.

Talking about our plans,
he says,
out in nature.

But, darling, I say,
you can't do that to the Cub Scouts.
Check into a nice hotel.

I tell him about the ocean.

But, my Hon, he says,
there are no hotels in the ocean.

How, for my Ocean, I get all the good One Ocean Hotel stuff.

Andy,
if you could stop by,
hook up the printer,
we could go out for lunch
at the One Ocean Hotel,
which is, of course, Oceanfront.
Eat on the patio.
Facing the ocean.
The Summer Ale Battered Fish & Chips is
so good
you think you are in Ireland
or even Massachusetts.
That's what I always have.
I think you'd like it, too.
Leaving, explain
our toddler nephew's
name
is
Ocean
and that we need for him
some
One Ocean small notepads,
some
One Ocean pencils,
some
One Ocean small blue (like Tiffany) bags
and,
of course,
some

One Ocean tissue paper.
Don't know why they don't have pens.
There should be
One Ocean
pens.

p.s.
There now are One Ocean pens,
They are very nice pens.

Things We Can't Talk About.

Outside. Writing.
My upstairs neighbor, Bill, a man, happens by.
I scream. Scream my fucking head off.
This happens every day. Sometimes, more than once.

I'm so sorry, Bill, I say. I'm so sorry.

It's ok, he says.
Your screams remind me of being in Vietnam.

Oh, Bill, no, I say,
you were in Vietnam.

I can't talk about that, Bill says.

And, I can't talk about why
when a man happens by I
scream.

That Object #2

So, see
what happened is
Andy wrote in a note one
of those words people use
for that object
and
(innocently,
he's new at this
no idea no clue
this is his introduction
to the word Minefield Spell
as time goes by
Andy becomes quite very aware of
Minefields
and
his intention was sweet
something like
he hated that
that part of his body
could be used
to so hurt a woman
something like that)
but
I got upset
very upset
sort of crazy
and
stayed crazy about it
days, a week, maybe a week and a half,
maybe longer, I hope not but

probably longer
even had a vision of one
that lived for a while
mid-air out on the patio
by the table where I write
that was hell
it was very bright pink very large
at first I didn't think anything of that
but at some point I realised they
do not come bright pink
they are flesh toned
and none of them are that big
once it followed along side the car
flying with me
all the way home from school
on that road where
I have to switch lanes
and
maintain a speed I am not
comfortable with
I think after that that's
maybe when
I went on
the medical leave.
I never saw it again
after that.
But I remember.
I remember.
Fearing descended into actual
madness
I talk with Donald about it.
This is normal he says.
Jung had visions.

I don't tell Donald,
do you really think anyone thinks
Jung was normal.
I do tell Donald
I do not find this helpful.

Andy and Janet do the math.

Math gave up on me when
the take-aways were introduced
First Grade.

Janet who can do math in her head
(both of her parents were physicists)
figures out the percentage of my life
I lived dead. She tells me either 40%
or less than 40%. I forget which.
I was thinking more like half. Sure
seemed longer than 40 or less %.

Andy who knows how to make pastry
which requires precision figures out the
actual number of days I lived dead.
I'm sure I wrote the number down but
can't right now find but haven't really looked
but it was something I think like only
something like over 10,000 days and it
seems to me I lived more days dead.
Dead. Circling. Circling. Dead.
It was kind of them. And, I appreciate it.
Doesn't make me feel any better.

37-years-old I died on my own
living room floor. Stayed
dead over 26 years. I know that's
a lot of math to do. A lot of ways
to do the math.

Context: Me & Bill

Night. Outside smoking.
Bill happens along by.
Hi, Bill, I call.
Bill stops.
You did not scream, he says.
I know, Bill, I did not scream.
That's great, he says.
Yes, I say, it's great.

Several now years ago
Bills moves in upstairs.
First morning day
I am outside reading.
He comes by up to me.
I'm Bill, he maybe says.
I can not believe this man is speaking to me.
Do not respond.
Despising Bill commences.
Next day morning
he does it again.
Really really despising Bill commences.

I maybe then small scream begin
when he everytime happens along by
not sure but think so.
(And, this was way before the real episode)

One day, a couple of years ago now
struggling with overweight huge suitcase
Bills is there and he helps me.

Puts easy into the back seat.
I think, My Goodness.
Bill really is a perfectly lovely man.

Still, I continue to I think small scream.
(Bill may have differing notion
how small the small screams.)

During the recent episode
maybe for around 3 months
when my sister's man dog walker
or of course Bill happen by
I scream my head off hell loud screams.

Finally, I just stop screaming.
Maybe just all screamed out.
(Still of course make the in the night in my bed screaming screams.)

Saturday errand home
we have an actual conversation.
He is reading on his balcony.
What are you reading, Bill, I call up.
He holds up a hardcover Nelson DeMille.
A new one, I exclaim. Is it good.
Pretty good, Bill says.

Once, during the episode
me scream apologizing
Bill says, It's ok.
You know, I swim with sharks.

Waking While Dead/
Waking While Again Alive

When I was dead.
For years.
First Waking Thought.
Fuck.
I'm still alive.

That finally stopped.
Hope all given up.
For the die-in-your-sleep
Actual Death.

This morning.
I leap hop out of bed.
Feet still in air.
Not yet landed.
Think.
What A Great Day.

Re-open.

The wound re-opens.
After over 26 years.
I re-remember everything
again.
The pain is extreme.
I am taking it all apart
again. Each piece. Each part. Piece by piece. Part by Part.
some days
I can't stop
Re-remembering
this
moment.
some days
I can't stop
Re-remembering
that
moment.
The wound is so re-open.
The pain is again extreme.
And, I can't stop. The pain is now.
I am re-open
the wound re-opens
and
everything re-opens.

The Flying White Tiger Dream

In the big white bed
I am happy.
He is beside me beginning
to lean over down toward me.
I am happy.
He is coming slowly closer.
I am happy.
Closer now to my face
he changes.
Now, it is
a huge flying white tiger
lunge flying at me.
Huge wild mouth. Teeth.
I don't know what to do.
So,
I wake up.

Morning,
do not bother about flying and white,
look up bad tigers in dreams.
Face Your Fears.

Like that is ever going to happen.

Love & Whispers

Love & Whispers
Andy's note ends.

Do you end notes
to all your girls
Love & Whispers.

You are the only one in the world today.
Love & Whispers
is yours, my love, all
yours.

(I hope she likes this.)

She likes this.

Ann's Kitchen Sink Faucets

Ann likes to talk about her not so all that new
kitchen sink faucets.

(If you let her go on long enough she'll start to tell you all about the old
kitchen sink faucets.)

Aileen and me, we like to talk. Talk about rape. Talk about
sexual assault. Talk about rape. Talk about sexual assault.
Talk about rape. Talk about sexual assault.
Talk about. Talk about. Talk about it.

Tell me.

Tell me an Ocean story, Liz, I say.
Tell me an Ocean story.
I don't want to write/read/think
think about rape today.
Liz tells me a story
Oceans traces his name now
on school sentence strips his grandmother sends.
Sentence strips, I say. And, tracing.
I love tracing and sentence strips.
For a while, this morning, I do not think/write/read
about rape. I think about my Ocean
Tracing his name. Ocean. Ocean.

But, then, my legs begin
trembling, that shaking wild thing they sometimes do.
And, I want to wild run somewhere. In a
greenfield wild somewhere. Somewhere away.
From here. Away from where it happened.
Somewhere where it never happens. Never.
Where we all run. Free. And.
Everywhere is, where we run, always green.

The Wound Re-Opens

The wound re-opens

and

everything re-opens

    after being over 26 years dead.

I re-discover.

    First.

touch . . .

    water on my skin
       my hand on my arm

sight . . .

    the oh my god no mirror what has happened to me
      the reading interventionist narrow mustache
        he has had years and I have never before seen

taste . . .

canned corn is actually delicious

sound . . .

Baez, Cohen
endless in my mind and throat

scent . . .

expensive
French

I am overwhelmed

Overwhelmed
I begin again
to write.

Something Else.

There is something else,
we do not know
about the crane.

There is something else
we do know
about the crane.

It is proven:
They learn.
Have a learning process.
There is real evidence of this.

They learn. They
learn how to fly.

My darling, maybe,
we, too, can learn. Learn
how to fly. Fly. And, in
flying learn.
That would be something else.
That would be

Spontaneous Orgasm

So,
in the coming again alive everywhere time,
one night,
inside the bed,
below my waist,
something more than unusual strange is happening.
Frantic. Frenzy. Wild. Movement.
I do not know what is happening.
And, then, there is this tightening.
And, then there is this release.
What just happened to me, I think.
Then, I think, Oh, That was an orgasm.

At Ken and Ann's house,
(with the garden Redwood)
in the guest bathroom.
It happens again.
Using the fancy expensive so soft French,
I am sure, make-up brush, brushing
on maybe possibly French mineral powder,
feels so wonderful I just keep brushing,
brushing and it feels so wonderful.
And, it happens again.

Seeds. Threads.

We are
sewing our lives back together.
He is in,
of all places,
Buffalo.
I am here.
We share. Threads. Threads.
Seeding clouds
both
black and white.

A Letter to Love.

Love,

Isn't it just awful, love, that love
doesn't do anything. Doesn't help.
Can't cure. Can't cease sorrow, suffering.
Why is love so utterly useless. Why was
love ever invented when it can't do
anything, anything at all. I am so
angry with right now love I'd like to give love
the silent treatment. But, love wouldn't care.
Love wouldn't even notice. I suppose actually
all I can right now actually this actual morning do
is love you. Just keep, loving you. And,
Even, Yes, Yes.

Washing News.

I am now talking to her
When washing talk to her
Whisper small whispers to her.

My sister Sally says,
the streets of Paris are washed every day.

Rhythm Is The Key To Good Sex

(A Headline Poem)

Well,

That's discouraging.

Such A Painful Sight

So, one day,
after I regain sense of sight
out of shower
towelling
right arm raised high
mirror
glimpse
my underarm
my hairless underarm
hairless
heartbroken shocked
when did this happen
for over 26 years
have lived dead
never looking/seeing
my own body
I loved
my underarm hair
soft and fluffy

Air. Slanting In/On.

Light mist morning rain.
Slants in
&
there is movement
in the air.
Finds somehow
my neck.

I like the way this early air
feels along my neck.

Want more.

Maybe. Maybe.

Is it possible,
Janet says,
Ray died.

And,
that is why
you
can be alive again.

Something I Like To Look At

Well, used to.
Maybe now again might.
From elbow onto hand.
Furry lots of male hair.

I used to like to look at that.
And, dream. Dream.

Addiction

Addiction,
my social worker cousin Janet
writes/says
is
flight
from unbearable truth.

I don't know if she made that up
herself
or
read it somewhere.

And, maybe that isn't exactly
what she says
but
something like that.

The problem is
it doesn't work. Addiction does not work.
Nothing
really works.
No roundtrip
tickets
available.
Nobody ever gets
to fly home.

Somehow
it's always middle of a Wednesday night
or about to be

What day is it, I say.
Wednesday, Donald says.
Oh, no, I say.
Donald says,
Tomorrow,
it will be Thursday.

I do not find this helpful.

Error.

(A Law & Order: Special Victims Unit Poem)

The Special is/was a mistake.
But, you can't blame the cast for that.
(Maybe the original writers. I don't know.
Maybe New York City.)

I know what Special means.
So do you.

A Special dessert.
A Special dress.
A Special on lamb chops.

There are no Special Victims.
Do you feel Special, Lillian.
I know I, I don't feel so Special.

Special is not the right word.

It should be
Law & Order: TVU.

Law & Order: Torture Victims Unit.

We're not Special.
We were tortured.
We are tortured.

What do you think, Lillian.

Seen/Spoken Simple Language Words Become Utter Sheer Lasting Hell.

Wednesday.

    Now, that's a real bad word.

Comb.

    Is a very bad word.

Baby

    Is a terrible bad word.

Woman

    Oh, that's a bad one.
    Why didn't he call me a person.
    Not Woman. Bothers me a lot he
    would ever even think of me as one of those.
    A Woman. Oh, and, No, once, he called me
    a Girl. A funny Girl. My funny girl. Oh. Oh.

My Love. My Dear.

    Well, that just annihilate crucifies.
    Don't want to talk about that.
    Can't talk about that.
    Oh, my. Oh, my.

Ocean's Imagination

Ocean who is now newly four
tells me the story
of when he was nine
and a sea urchin
bit his foot
right here on this patio
it hurt so much
he could not drive
and
went to the hospital in a ambulance.

Now, he begins to tell me
about when he was eighteen in Australia
his experience there with the there sea urchin
but he doesn't finish that story
Cinderella
Is on TV.

Fear Is Always

Jamie posts
Fear is always about the future.

I don't think so. Lillian,
do you think so. I just
don't think so.

Question

in my notebook
I write
in the dead years not
but now alive again
no idea
what writing about
that I haven't taken
a bath in 27 years
I don't know
no idea
oh possibly Valentine's Day
today is Valentine's Day
I used to love Valentine's Day
starting to now
again yes
Happy Valentine's Day
Ocean and I make handmade
Valentine's Day Cards
Construction Paper Markers Small Red Heart Stickers
I fold for him the paper
Teach Ocean to write the word Love
Teach Ocean to spell the word Love

27th February 11

My niece gives me
a small black gift bag
tied with good black ribbon
inside a love card, chocolates, bubbles.
On top a note
What do you give someone for this
kind of anniversary.
This is my first gift for this
kind of anniversary.
My niece knows something about this
kind of anniversary.

Trying Not To Think About Thursday.
Today is Tuesday morning.

Do you like him.
Mother is asking me about the dentist.
Is he gentle.

I had 3 appointments last week.
Xrays.
Cleaning.
Something else hideous I don't want to think about can't think
the name for.

I say,
I don't know.
I really didn't see him last week.
Someone else did the Xrays.
Someone else did the cleaning.

Then, I remember.
He did have his hands in my mouth.
On more than one occasion. He did.
I blanked out I guess. (The way I blanked
out the times after I tried heterosexual
intercourse.) I don't
remember
what it felt like
to have his hands in my mouth.
And,
Thursday, he very much will
will have his hands in my mouth.
That's why he prescribed

the Xanax tablets
to take before the Thursday
hands in my mouth time.

Today is Tuesday morning.
I have to today take care of a 4-year-old.
I can't think about the dentist.
Can't
think about hands.
Hands inside my mouth.

We'll make handmade Easter cards.
Learn to write, spell
Happy with a capital H.
Hope I blank again out Thursday.
You can't you know always count on
blanking out when you need to blank out.
Thank God for Tablets with a capital T.

A hotel would be involved.

I want to have an affair,
I tell Andy,
with my new dentist.

But, my Hon, Andy says,
what would he do with his hands.

Well, Andy, I say,
there is that.
I was more focused on the 24-hour room service.
And, in the spa, the unlimited free champagne.

I want to have an affair,
I tell Liz,
with my new dentist.

Hon, Liz says,
I'm a little confused.
I thought you're a lesbian.
Elizabeth, I say, I am a lesbian.
I'm just not a very good lesbian.

You're my funny lesbian.
Andy says.
Waves his hands at me. Laughs.

The Unpredictable Vulva

In my experience,

Andy says,

the response of the vulva

is hard to predict.

Yeah.
Mine, too. Mine, too.
Yeah.

Days

Days return to being days
after being for sometime something
else I can not name but know
is not/was not Days

A bunny for Honey

My Ocean tells his mother
he wants her
to draw
a bunny for Honey.
And,
he will color the bunny for Honey in.
She does.
My Ocean in turquoise crayon
top of the bunny for Honey paper
prints
in all capital letters
C A D O A
My Ocean
colors the bunny for Honey
blue, his favorite color, and raspberry.
His mother
colors in the inner bunny for Honey ears
in yellow.
I know this because
no a few days four-year-old
colors in inner bunny for Honey ears
like that.
Bottom of the a bunny for Honey paper
my Ocean's mother prints
in pencil
A bunny for Honey
Below that
when I get my a bunny for Honey paper
I print
Charlotte, NC October
he is just now 4.

Real Life & Romance Novels

For years, nights my women family members
(the men all sound sleep through anything)
have stayed inside their beds listening to me
scream. Scream for hours.

In romance novels, pretty often this happens.
Someone in the night screams.

In romance novels,
the about to become lover always
goes to the screamer, the screamer
wakes, stops screaming, then something
nice always happens because
it's a romance novel.

In romance novels, when the lovers
begin to sleep together inside the same bed,
the screamer never again screams because
it's a romance novel.

My life is not a romance novel.

My Ocean

For my Ocean, I enter the ocean.
Hold him high when the big waves come.
Together, we work on our rhyming words.
And, our beginning letter sounds.
Outside, we paint.
Hang Ocean's paintings from the courtyard Japanese plum.
Make a sign.
Our signs says
Ocean's Art Show.

Finding Milk. Most Likely Whole.

Andy write poems
so full of surprises
you might even find
inside one an unexpected
unexplained
glass of milk.

Dream. February 22.

small New England town
white painted houses
porch swings and porches and
swings for children under shade trees
you just happen upon
on a woods walk and can't resist

in this quiet place where I am
where I live most quietly
you find me you
begin to tell to me your story
all night you tell me your story
pieces bits parts in
nothing resembling any kind of actual order
side by side on porch swings, side by side
leaning back into porch railings, swaying a little
side by side on swings for children
telling your eyes look only down
listening my eyes swallow sorrow
when I wake I know
you had/have more story to tell
I'd been in bed then such a long time
I am sorry love even for you I
could not stay longer

the porch swings and porches bright white
our outfits bright white
no hats no snacks
the sitting part of the swings for children
blood bright red

Dreams Picnic

Andy cannot come. So,
he writes.

You always shine at picnics.
You will be the sunflower girl.
And, the picnic will live forever.

Mothers and children come.
Hold fast tight in my arms children.
Hand mothers Dream poems.

Try not to cry.

March 20.

Wake. happy. laughing.
Liz is calling out to me
Honeybunney. Honeybunney.
It's time to work on the poems.

Happy to find
a happy good morning email from Andy.

But,
the email is not from Andy.
The email is from Andy's son Benjamin.

Urgent. Please phone.

Just tell me, Benjamine, I write.
Just Tell Me.

Afternoon,
I tell Elizabeth,
this changes the book.
No, Liz, says,
maybe this changes the dedication.
This does not change the book.

No, Liz, I say,
this does not change the dedication.
This changes the book.

The book changes.

Wednesday, March 19

Featured artwork of the day:
A sculpture of child Saint Agnes.

I look up Aries March 19 horoscopes.

One. Watch morale.

Another. Things are going wrong.

Another. Tomorrow, the sun moves into the springtime
sign of Aries with a promise.

Another. Keep a notebook by your bed to record
dreams.

But, there are no dreams to record.

Estimated time of death,
Andy's son Benjamin tells me,
is between 6 and 7 pm.

Agnes is the patron saint of gardeners
and
child rape victims.

Soon, he would have become 52.

No note has yet been found.

Only poems.

Floating While Revolving and Floating While Inside The Sea

we revolve
revolve and float in air
and
we are inside the sea
floating inside the sea

inside the dreamworld
we go back and forth
floating while revolving
high in balmy air
no net
floating while inside the sea
deep inside the sea
no net

inside the dreamworld
we are both together comfortable
floating beside one another
wherever we are floating
although in real life you are not
comfortable in the ocean
and
in real life I am not at all
comfortable with heights

we are not visible

(although once I perhaps
glimpsed your curving bright hair

side of your face as we were
re-entering a revolving time)

I just know we are together
beside one another floating

no talking. no outfits.
just invisible hearts holding hands

inside the dreamworld
I believe you are still with me
in the now real life world

and
inside the dreamworld
I know you are no longer
alive with me in this world you
have left me to be alone
to be without

I do not want to wake.
I want to stay inside the dreamworld
with you
floating. revolving.
with you.

hon, hard you know, hon
to live without, hon.
without.

His favorite place.

Andy's daughter Olivia says,
I do not know his favorite place.

Liv, love, I say,
Your father's favorite place
was/is anyplace/everyplace
he ever held you in his arms.

Ignition. Without batteries.

He ignites my post traumatic stress episode.
He ignites my coming alive again.
He ignites my again writing.

Also,

he ignites my heart.

And,

we both sort of fall fall
fast and so unexpectedly
fast fall into

And,

in the falling, I get
a little scared well more than a little
And, I don't know what to do.
So, I tell him I'm a lesbian.
And, unfortunately, he believes me.
I must have been very convincing.
Of course, it's true I am a lesbian but
that's so sort of not the point and
I'm not a very good lesbian.

You're my funny girl, he says.
My funny lesbian.

And,

so, then, the Minefield Word Spells stop.

And,

so, then,
the post traumatic episode stops.

And, so, then, he dies.

Not the expected heroin death.
The unexpected/expected suicide death.

This is not a made-for-tv movie on Lifetime the women's network.

Unfortunately, this is real life and true.

He dies.

He was.

He was a poet.

He was a pastry chef.
The simple things, he loved best making.
creme brulee.

He was a nurse.
But, there were all those cabinets.
With all that injectable morphine.

He did something with computers.
I don't understand because

He was a poet.

He was.

Darling

I loved you

more than seaglass.

His last March 19 words to me.

Love you, Hon. Love you

The End.

I finished the book, I tell Bill.

That's great, Bill says.
Hope you make tons of money.

Oh, Bill, I say,
it's poetry.
Not Nelson DeMille.

Andy Reads Me A Poem.

Wildberry pomegranate.
It's a powdered fruit drink.
I love it.

Is that the, um, poem, I say.

No, Hon, that was me making a drink.

This is the poem.

A NOTE ABOUT THE AUTHOR

Frances Driscoll grew up in New England. She is the author of two collections of poems: *Talk to Me* (Gillian Conoley's Black River Press) and *The Rape Poems* (Jack Estes' Pleasure Boat Studio) and is published widely in literary journals. William Slaughter's Mudlark published a chapbook of *The Rape Poems*.

Frances Driscoll's work is used by trauma therapists, social workers, sexual assault awareness trainings for the U.S. Air Force and U.S. National Guard. Her work is taught in a number of schools in a variety of disciplines, adapted for several stage productions, and is the subject of Justine Gieni's University of Regina English master's thesis, "Hysterical (r)evoluton: The Creation of Embodied Language" and Amy Griffiths' University of Minnesota English Ph.D. dissertation, "In a Shattered Language: a feminist poetics of trauma."

You can hear Driscoll read some of *The Rape Poems* and *Seaglass Picnic* poems at Mark Ari's Eat-Magazine.com.

A NOTE ABOUT THE TYPE

This book is set in Garamond, a typeface originally designed by the Parisian type cutter Claude Garamond (c. 1500–61). The Garamond types are clear, open, and elegant.

·

Poetry Books from *Pleasure Boat Studio: A Literary Press*
Listed by release date

The following books are from Empty Bowl Press, a Division of Pleasure Boat Studio

Swimming the Colorado ~ Denise Banker
Lessons Learned ~ Finn Wilcox
Petroglyph Americana ~ Scott Ezell
Old Tale Road ~ Andrew Schelling
Working the Woods, Working the Sea ~ Eds. Finn Wilcox, Jerry Gorsline
The Blossoms Are Ghosts at the Wedding ~ Tom Jay ~ with essays
Desire ~ Jody Aliesan
Dreams of the Hand ~ Susan Goldwitz
The Basin: Poems from a Chinese Province ~ Mike O'Connor
The Straits ~ Michael Daley
In Our Hearts and Minds: The Northwest and Central America ~ Ed. Michael Daley
The Rainshadow ~ Mike O'Connor
Untold Stories ~ William Slaughter

Our Chapbook Series

No. 1: *The Handful of Seeds: Three and a Half Essays* ~ Andrew Schelling
No. 2: *Original Sin* ~ Michael Daley
No. 3: *Too Small to Hold You* ~ Kate Reavey
No. 4: *The Light on Our Faces* ~ re-issued in non-chapbook (see previous list)
No. 5: *Eye* ~ William Bridges
No. 6: *Selected New Poems of Rainer Maria Rilke* ~ trans. fm German by Alice Derry
No. 7: *Through High Still Air: A Season at Sourdough Mountain* ~ Tim McNulty
No. 8: *Sight Progress* ~ Zhang Er, trans. from Chinese by Rachel Levitsky
No. 9: *The Perfect Hour* ~ Blas Falconer
No. 10: *Fervor* ~ Zaedryn Meade
No. 11: *Some Ducks* ~ Tim McNulty
No. 12: *Late August* ~ Barbara Brackney
No. 13: *The Right to Live Poetically* ~ Emily Haines

From other publishers (in limited editions)

In Blue Mountain Dusk ~ Tim McNulty ~ Broken Moon Press
China Basin ~ Clemens Starck ~ Story Line Press
Journeyman's Wages ~ Clemens Starck ~ Story Line Press

Orders: Pleasure Boat Studio books are available by order from your bookstore, directly from our website, or through the following:
SPD (Small Press Distribution) Tel. 800-869-7553, Fax 510-524-0852
Partners/West Tel. 425-227-8486, Fax 425-204-2448
Baker & Taylor Tel. 800-775-1100, Fax 800-775-7480
Ingram Tel. 615-793-5000, Fax 615-287-5429
Amazon.com or **Barnesandnoble.com**

Pleasure Boat Studio: A Literary Press
201 West 89th Street
New York, NY 10024
www.pleasureboatstudio.com / pleasboat@nyc.rr.com

CPSIA information can be obtained
at www.ICGtesting.com
Printed in the USA
FSOW04n1711261215
14643FS

9 780912 887418